LET'S ALL SHUT UP

AND

MAKE MONEY!

Hong Kong's final 100 days
under British colonial rule

written and illustrated by
Larry Feign

To CHRISTOPHER —

H BEST WISHES FROM

Larry Feign

Cartoons on pages 51-54 reprinted by kind permission of *Time Magazine*.

ISBN 962 7866 13 X

Published by

Hambalan Press
GPO Box 6086
Hong Kong

http://www.asiaonline.net/lilywong/hambalan.htm

Printed in the Hong Kong Special Administrative Region of the People's Republic of China

This book was produced entirely on a **COMPAQ** computer. Who needs Macs for publishing?

Contents

once again, for Cathy

Author's note

This book is a complete collection of "The World of Lily Wong" cartoons drawn during Hong Kong's last 100 days under British colonial rule.

Lily Wong satirised life and politics in Hong Kong for over ten years. She debuted in the *Hongkong Standard* in 1986 and moved the following year to the *South China Morning Post*, where she showed up on page 2 six days a week. That is, until the feature was abruptly terminated in May 1995 after a series of cartoons which insulted Chinese communist leaders (see the book *Banned In Hong Kong* for the whole story).

In March 1997 I was commissioned by the British newspaper *The Independent* to chronicle, with cartoons, Hong Kong's final 100 days as a British colony. Naturally, Lily Wong was employed for the task.

The cartoons were produced in Hong Kong and then sent, via the miracle of the Internet, directly from my Lantau Island home to the London Docklands. There are not 100 of them, because the feature appeared only Monday-Friday. However, this book includes other cartoons drawn during the same period or which are relevant to the topic.

The colour section on pages 51-54 was done for *Time Magazine* in May 1997, and "The Kowloon Kats" was published in 1995 in *Geo*. The History cartoons are previously unpublished. The cartoon on page 21 won the Amnesty International 1997 Human Rights Press Award.

Thanks

My heartfelt thanks to Mr Andrew Marr, Editor of *The Independent*, for having the eccentric notion of publishing in his newspaper a daily cartoon about a place seven time zones away. Special thanks also to Andrew Marshall, Foreign Editor, for contacting me in the first place and campaigning hard for this project, to Steve Crawshaw and Steven Vines for their assistance, and particularly to Jojo Moyes, who originally suggested the idea.

Acknowledgement also to the anonymous "Mr Lee" for his passionate remarks, some of which I have incorporated into the History chapter, and to Skip Press, writer extraordinaire, for his sensitive editing of my untrained prose.

Love and gratitude as usual to my dear wife Cathy for her constant support, her insights and opinions—not always in agreement with mine—and for reading and editing every cartoon in this book before it left the drawing table. Finding the tolerance to live with a cartoonist (or is it just me?) is one of the world's great unreported challenges.

A politically incorrect history of Hong Kong

There's a riddle going around Hong Kong: If the British were responsible for Hong Kong's success, then why aren't all of their colonies and former colonies rich? The reply, of course, is that Hong Kong was actually built by the blood, sweat and cleverness of its Chinese inhabitants. Good riddance to the colonial tyrants who brought nothing but shame upon China.

Those nasty Brits

Britain had undeniably despicable motives in colonising Hong Kong. The Opium War broke out because British drug dealers, backed by London, insisted on breaking China's laws against importing opium and exporting silver. China lost the battle with the barbarians, ceded territory and changed its national laws under duress. This opened the door to other foreign powers swarming in to grab "concessions": quasi-colonial enclaves inside China's main trading ports. The result was the worst humiliation China had endured in hundreds of years, something not easily forgotten.

British rule in Hong Kong has not been a shining example of egalitarianism and democracy. They weren't here to

do anyone a favour. The governor ruled as a benign dictator, appointed by London. On the other hand, any governor who showed the slightest inclination to improve conditions for the Chinese was quickly hounded out by the local British taipans. As recently as 1988 all members of the legislature were appointed by the governor.

Racism, corruption and exploitation were integral parts of the system well into the 1970s. When I arrived in Hong Kong in 1985 I was shocked at the archaic colonialist attitudes I found among white people here (and not just among Brits). Until a policy of localisation was finally implemented in the 1980s, the colour of one's skin seemed to be of much more importance than expertise in securing employment, promotion and stratospheric salary levels, in private enterprise and government alike.

Not until 1990 did the colonial government even began to pay lip service to the political wishes and ambitions of local Chinese people. Only during its last five years of administering its colony did Britain try to make amends and give Hong Kong people a genuine voice in their own affairs. Too little, too late.

That's one way of looking at Hong Kong's history, and the part that will remain in local textbooks. Here's what they'll leave out:

The British brought to Hong Kong—as to all of their colonies—the rule of law and an impartial judicial system. From the first day of British rule, Chinese people living in

Hong Kong enjoyed a degree of civil liberties that they have never experienced in China at any time in its history.

Rule of law meant contracts and property rights were protected. That, a non-interventionist, *laisser-faire* style of government, and the establishment of Hong Kong as a free port, sowed the seeds for Hong Kong to quickly become the easiest place on earth to do business.

Since the 1970s corruption in Hong Kong government and private enterprise has been virtually wiped out by the British, leaving Hong Kong about the least corrupt place in Asia. The government has been "localised", resulting in an efficient, orderly civil service where promotion is based entirely on merit, unlike the system across the border fence. Freedom of speech, religion and the press have been the most wide-ranging in Asia (despite an epidemic of self-censorship during the past few years, which is not Britain's doing).

Most important of all, Hong Kong was a tiny bastion of stability while mainland China underwent revolution, upheaval, civil war, famine and almost non-stop repression under three regimes during the past century and a half.

The role of the Chinese

Economically, Chinese people built Hong Kong. They provided the labour, were the middle-men between foreign traders and China, and aside from the leading British firms (today mostly Chinese-owned and managed),

CHINA'S EVOLVING ATTITUDE

Chinese established most of the businesses.

At the time Britain took over, in 1841, there were only a few hundred Chinese people living on Hong Kong island. Like the British, most Chinese people in the colony came later. Millions of them.

95% of Hong Kong residents are either refugees from China or the children of refugees. Almost all have arrived since 1949. They still arrive at a rate of over 150 legal immigrants per day, and countless illegals. Almost all have been farm workers from neighbouring Guangdung (Canton) Province, coming here either to escape from China or to exploit the opportunities that Hong Kong offers, usually both. They came not because Hong Kong was British, but because it was a separate entity from China, a stable enclave where rule of law and economic freedom prevailed.

This is Hong Kong's history in a nutshell: cynical in origin, mercenary in nature, established by scoundrels, populated by peasants. And which has become one of the most outstanding, successful and magnetic cities on earth.

Hong Kong's history (revised version)

In the several months leading up to the change in sovereignty, Beijing's propaganda masters did an excellent job of putting a positive spin on the handover by encouraging pride and patriotism among Hong Kong Chinese people. Hong Kong has returned to the Motherland! The shame of colonialism has been eradicated!

This would be laudable if they stopped there. But they have gone leagues beyond that, encouraging nationalism (defined as "patriotism without conscience") and a sneering racial superiority complex. But most disturbing to myself and many intellectual Chinese people I know is the new, revisionist history being promoted.

This revisionist view blandly states that Chinese people alone built Hong Kong, while the British were at best, irrelevant, or at worst, brutal tyrants. In other words, had Hong Kong never been colonised, it would still be the glittering, wealthy, bustling commercial metropolis that it is today. The great international trading centre known as Hong Kong was stolen by Britain, and Hong Kong's infrastructure, its buildings, its institutions and its treasury are at last being returned to its rightful owner.

Which is obviously utter nonsense.

If Britain had never been here, Hong Kong would today be nothing more than a sparsely-populated collection of fishing villages, no different than any of the other islands and inlets along the south China coast. There would never have been a place of refuge and opportunity. There would be no skyscrapers, no fancy new airport, no container port. And there would certainly not be 6½ million people.

Where would they all be? Several thousands might have fled China by going abroad. But most would be back on the farm in China, where they or their parents came from, knee-deep in mud and dung! As ugly as this

1982: THE DECISION TO TAKE BACK HONG KONG

HOW TO NEGOTIATE WITH THE CHINESE

THE RIGHT WAY
RULE #1: NEVER LET THE OTHER SIDE LOSE FACE.

NICE SHIRT. GREAT BOOZE! SAY, BY THE WAY, YOU KNOW THAT 99-YEAR LEASE? WHAT IF MAYBE IT WERE EXTENDED...?

OH. HA HA. SURE, WHY NOT?

THE WRONG WAY
SEND THATCHER

HONG KONG IS NOW AND FOREVER BRITISH!

YOU DIE!!

may sound to a designer-suited Hong Kong Chuppie (Chinese Yuppie) sitting over a bowl of overpriced, nutritionless shark fin soup, shouting into a mobile phone to his or her stockbroker or bookie, it's the truth and at this time of reflection over the transfer of sovereignty, it needs to be acknowledged.

Yes, colonialism is indefensible and Britain's departure was inevitable. But let's admit that without the British, Hong Kong would be *nothing*. The neighbouring manufacturing zone of Shenzhen wouldn't exist, and the city of Guangzhou—indeed the whole of south China—would never have prospered without British Hong Kong. China itself would be a very different place had it not been for the vast amounts of money, expertise and technology that have flowed into China from British Hong Kong.

Hong Kong has also been a safe haven for Chinese political refugees, including Dr Sun Yat-sen, founder of modern China. Even the communist regime in China has British Hong Kong to thank for its very survival. From the 1950s through the 1970s, while the United States-led embargo on China kept it isolated from much of the world, Hong Kong was the mainland's major conduit for imports, exports and vital foreign exchange.

It might hurt to admit, but the foreign devil British have, unintentionally, had a highly positive effect on 20th Century Chinese history, merely by possessing and governing Hong Kong. They deserve neither thanks nor jeers. But they do deserve a bit of credit.

What do they get instead? Demands to apologise for

the shame of the Opium War, which happened over 150 years ago. But what about more recent shames brought upon the Chinese people, such as the Great Leap Forward, only 40 years ago, in which Mao's insane policies directly caused tens of millions of Chinese people to starve to death? What about the Cultural Revolution, which ended just over 20 years ago, in which children turned on their parents, an entire generation was lost and 5000 years of Chinese civilisation nearly wiped out? Only 9 years ago tanks and armoured personnel carriers (the same type driven into Hong Kong by the PLA on the day of the handover) gunned down and ran over peaceful students, peasants and workers in Tiananmen Square.

Aren't these events as shameful and humiliating to the Chinese people as the Opium Wars, in which few died and a tiny scrap of almost uninhabited territory was temporarily lost? Shouldn't such atrocities, committed within living memory by the government now in charge of Hong Kong, be of more concern to all Chinese people than the actions of the British who, having won a long-ago battle, ushered in a century and a half of peace, freedom and prosperity to this little domain?

Ironically, nowadays the international trade in opium-based narcotics is dominated by Chinese triad societies, who in just the past few years have been labelled "patriots" and "people we can work with" by Chinese government officials. Shouldn't the vilification of long-dead 19th Century British opium traders be redirected toward China itself for this present-day menace?

1980s: SINO-BRITISH NEGOTIATIONS

OUR FIRST PRIORITY IS TO PRESERVE THE RIGHTS AND FREEDOMS OF HONG KONG PEOPLE.

HEY, WE'RE PLANNING THIS NUCLEAR POWER PLANT. THINK A BRITISH CONSORTIUM MIGHT WANT A PIECE OF THE ACTION?

NO ONE WILL NOTICE JUST ONE OR TWO ITSY-BITSY LITTLE WORDS MISSING.

1990s: BRITAIN'S FAREWELL GIFT TO HONG KONG

The new colony of Hong Kong

What gets lost in everyone's histories is that Hong Kong people have created a great and miraculous city without ever having had any control over their own destiny. As colonial subjects, local people were never even remotely in charge. During Sino-British negotiations in the 1980s, Hong Kong people were excluded from all discussions, at the insistence of the Chinese government. Even the handover ceremony itself was conduced entirely in British English and Mandarin, both foreign languages here. Not a single word was in Cantonese, the native dialect of 98% of Hong Kong residents. The people of Hong Kong seem to have switched from one colonial master to another.

Little has changed yet in Hong Kong except the flags and the postage stamps (and the unconstitutional "provisional legislature" appointed by Beijing). As usual, the future is entirely up to the Chinese people of Hong Kong, in spite of their government. Let's hope they are mature enough to get past the sloganeering, nationalism and racism, and to lead themselves and the whole of China to a brighter, more humane and democratic future.

The last
100 days

EXCUSE ME! 98 DAYS UNTIL HONG KONG'S HANDOVER. HOW OPTIMISTIC ARE YOU?

AS OPTIMISTIC AS CAN BE, KNOWING THAT A BUNCH OF WRINKLED OLD DICTATORS ARE ABOUT TO TAKE OVER AND SEND IN THE SAME ARMY THAT SLAUGHTERED ITS OWN CITIZENS IN TIANANMEN SQUARE.

SORRY, SIR. WE CAN'T LET YOU SAY THAT ON TV.

WHY NOT? FREE SPEECH IS LEGAL!

YEAH, BUT SUICIDE ISN'T.

HEY, SIS. WHAT'S WITH HIM?

HE GOT FIRED FOR MAKING SOME ANTI-CHINA REMARK.

POOR STUART! NO ONE IN HONG KONG WILL HIRE HIM! ALL HE CAN DO IS LIE AROUND DRINKING AND WATCHING TV ALL DAY.

HEY, BOSS — JIANG ZEMIN IS A POO-POO HEAD.

Pay-n-Weep SUPERMARKET

MEGA BUCKS

FEIGN

SINO-
BRITISH
JOINT
LIAISON
GROUP

THE
DIPLOMATS
ARE **IN**

HI. I'M THE HONG KONG GOVERNMENT SECRETARY, SENT HERE TO—

BOW TO CHAIRMAN MAO, THEN **CONFESS**, YOU REVISIONIST SCUM COUNTER-REVOLUTIONARY COW-DEMON IMPERIALIST RUNNING DOG!!

ER...COMRADE...THIS IS *1997*, NOT 1967 CULTURAL REVOLUTION

DID I DO IT AGAIN? TSK. I HATE GETTING OLD.

WHAT THE—?

Pay 'n' Weep SUPERMARKET

"TRANSFER of SOVEREIGNTY" SALE

LOOK AT THAT QUEUE! WHAT'S GOING ON, WONG?

WELL, BOSS— REMEMBER ALL THEM DUSTY JARS OF HP SAUCE AND (RETCH!) MARMITE THAT WE CAN'T EVEN GIVE AWAY?

INVEST NOW!

COLONIAL ERA COLLECTOR'S ITEMS

LAST CHANCE before the HANDOVER!

Limit 5 per customer

RUDY, YOU'RE A GENIUS!

FEIGN

AND SO THE GOVERNMENT IS GETTING RID OF ALL COLONIAL SYMBOLS.

Hong Kon
Governme
Dept. of
PREVARICAT
and
USCATIO

EVERY REMINDER OF BRITISH IMPERIAL RULE IS TO BE DISPOSED OF.

DID THEY DUMP THE GOVERNOR'S ROLLS-ROYCE YET?

GOVT
HOUSE

FEIGN

THIS DRAFT PUBLIC ORDER BILL FORBIDS POLITICAL PARTIES FROM ACCEPTING DONATIONS FROM "ALIENS".*

PUBLIC ORDER BILL

Provisional Legislature of HKSAR

EVEN A SINGLE "ALIEN" DONATION GETS THE WHOLE PARTY IN TROUBLE.

WHY WOULD CHINA— UH OH.

* ACTUAL WORDING OF CONSULTATION PAPER

HEH HEH

READY... AIM...

DEMOCRAT PARTY of HONG KONG

FEIGN

EXCUSE ME, AVERAGE HONG KONG CITIZEN. DO YOU THINK THERE'LL BE FREEDOM OF SPEECH HERE AFTER THE HANDOVER?

ABSOLUTELY.

FOR THE FIRST TIME IN YEARS AND YEARS, PEOPLE WILL BE FREE...

...TO TALK ABOUT SOMETHING BESIDES "WHAT'S GOING TO HAPPEN AFTER THE HANDOVER?"

HONG KONG 1997: A TIME OF GREAT UNCERTAINTY

WHEN FREEDOM OF SPEECH, PRESS AND BELIEF, RULE OF LAW - INDEED AN ENTIRE WAY OF LIFE - ARE ON THE LINE

A TIME WHEN ALL 6.3 MILLION PEOPLE IN HONG KONG ARE PREOCCUPIED WITH A SINGLE OVERRIDING THOUGHT ...

HOW CAN I CASH IN ON THIS?

SEE? I GOT TOYS— LIKE TRANSFORMER CADRE® JUST FLIP THIS...

AND HE TRANSFORMS INTO A CAPITALIST!

...AND VICE-VERSA!

I GOT FASHION — SPECIALLY FOR SEEING THE NEWS: CONFIDENCE BUILDERS™ ROSE-COLORED GLASSES!

AND MY PIÈCE DE RÉSISTANCE...

WAI! YOU AIN'T MY GRANDMA!

HEH-HEH. I ATE HER.

O GASP! O MOAN! I SHALL CALL THE HUNTER, WHO WILL SPLIT YOU ASUNDER (HEY, ALMOST RHYMES) AND GET BACK MY DEAR OLD GRAN—

YOU WOULDN'T, IF YOU KNEW HOW MUCH THIS PROPERTY COULD FETCH.

Property News

CHINA CONSORTIUM BID FOR SEVEN DWARF COTTAGE

"SO RED RIDING HOOD AND THE WOLF BULLDOZED THE HOUSE, BUILT A 68-STOREY OFFICE COMPLEX, LAUNDERED THE MONEY THROUGH A BERMUDA SHELF COMPANY AND LIVED TAX-FREE EVER AFTER ON THE COSTA DEL SOL." LILY! WHO GOT HER THIS BOOK??

READ IT AGAIN!

LITTLE RED RIDING HOOD
Hong Kong Edition

FEIGN

LOOK AT CRYSTAL. SO ADORABLE!

HEY, SWEETIE. WHAT ARE ALL THOSE DOLLS DOING?

THOSE ARE THE DEMONSTRATORS.

AND HERE COMES THE PEOPLE'S LIBERATION ARMY! *WHEEEE!*

WHAT THE #@!!✳ ARE THEY TEACHING HER IN KINDER- GARTEN?!

HI. WE'RE CRYSTAL'S PARENTS. WE WANT TO KNOW ABOUT THIS PROPAGANDA SHE'S BEEN BRINGING HOME.

LUCKY GOLD Kindergarten

HA-HA. NOT PROPAGANDA.

HONG KONG SCHOOLS ARE JUST MAKING A FEW HARMLESS ADJUSTMENTS IN CURRICULUM, IN LINE WITH THE CHANGE IN SOVEREIGNTY. ALL IN GOOD FUN—

WING-LING! NOT HIM! THE EFFIGY OF CHRIS PATTEN IS OVER THERE!!

FEIGN

OKAY, CLASS. LET'S SEE WHO'S GOING TO BE "WEE HELPER" TODAY, TO PASS AROUND THE TRAY OF APPLE SLICES.

LUCKY GOLD Kindergarten

HOW DO YOU CHOOSE? PICK A CHILD'S NAME OUT OF A HAT?

OH, NO! HA HA!

WE FOLLOW THE DEMOCRATIC EXAMPLE OF OUR FUTURE CHIEF EXECUTIVE.

ALL RIGHT, BARNEY YEUNG IS HELPER...

OUT LI PENG

TO BE SHOT

FEIGN

OKAY, CHILDREN, WHO CAN TELL ME THE *TRUTH* ABOUT OUR HISTORY? BERNIE?

LUCKY GOLD Kindergarten

UM...THERE WERE THESE EVIL, NASTY BRITISHERS, WHO FORCED EVERYONE TO TAKE OPIUM, AND... AND THEY TOOK OVER HONG KONG.

GOOD. WHO CAN TELL ME ABOUT THE CHANGE IN SOVEREIGNTY? BETTY?

AND NOW THAT THE DOPE BUSINESS IS RUN BY PATRIOTIC CHINESE TRIADS, WE NO LONGER NEED THE BRITS!

FEIGN

63

WAH! BEIJING AND THE TRIADS IN CAHOOTS. WHY AIN'T I SURPRISED?

"OFFICIALS PROMISED TRIAD CHIEFS THEY WOULD TURN A BLIND EYE TO CRIMINAL ACTIVITIES IN RETURN FOR PROMISES NOT TO CAUSE TROUBLE DURING THE HANDOVER."*

HA! WONDER IF HONG KONG'S GOING ALONG WITH THAT?

JAYWALKER!!

*GENUINE NEWS ITEM

MR RUDY WONG, YOU ARE CHARGED WITH WILFUL AND PREMEDITATED JAYWALKING.

THE COURT NOTES THAT AMONGST EVIDENCE FILED IN YOUR OWN DEFENCE, YOU CITE THE LATE DENG XIAOPING.

HOWEVER, I BELIEVE DENG'S ACTUAL WORDS WERE: "IT DOESN'T MATTER WHETHER A CAT IS BLACK OR WHITE, AS LONG AS IT CATCHES MICE"

...NOT "IT DOESN'T MATTER WHETHER A TRAFFIC SIGNAL IS GREEN OR RED..."

DETAILS, DETAILS...

FEIGN

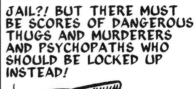

YES, MOTHER, I KNOW THERE ARE ONLY 36 DAYS LEFT.

MA, DON'T WORRY! HONG KONG IS CALM. IT'LL BE FINE! PEOPLE ARE JUST NERVOUS, THAT'S ALL.

THE TENSION HERE IS SO THICK YOU COULD... YOU COULD...

SHOOT IT IN THE BACK OF THE NECK WITH A KALISHNIKOV.

I HEARD THAT!!

THEY WON'T TOUCH FOREIGNERS, MA! THEY PROMISED!

FEIGN

HI. WE WANT TO ENQUIRE ABOUT IMMIGRATING TO AUSTRALIA.

AUSTRALIA

CONSULA

POMS SERVED AT WINDOW 14

YES, SIR. YOU SIMPLY COMPLETE THESE FORMS. THEN YOU'LL EACH NEED A HEALTH CHECK.

Fovm 47

SYDN 2000

...AND A STATEMENT OF CRIMINAL RECORD.

CRIMINAL RECORD?

I DIDN'T KNOW THAT WAS STILL MANDATORY!

FEIGN

EVERYONE, PLEASE MEET MR XI. HE TAKES OVER FROM ME AS DEPARTMENT HEAD AFTER THE HANDOVER.

Hong Kong Government Dept. of Prevarication and Obf...tion

WELCOME! LET'S ALL CELEBRATE WITH A LAVISH 12-COURSE BANQUET AT DEPARTMENT EXPENSE!

NOT HUNGRY, EH? THEN HOW ABOUT JUST PAYING ME THE CASH EQUIVALENT?

"ONE COUNTRY TWO SYSTEMS" WILL OBVIOUSLY HAVE SOME TEETHING PROBLEMS.

FEIGN

EXCUSE ME, MR XI, BUT THERE'S NO SMOKING IN THIS OFFICE.

HAH?

SEE? UNDER HONG KONG LAW, NO SMOKING, SPITTING OR GAMBLING IS ALLOWED IN ANY GOVERNMENT OFFICE.

LAWS of HONG KONG

WELL, THAT'S ONE MORE BIT OF COLONIALIST OPPRESSION WE'LL BE LIBERATED FROM ON JULY 1!

RRRRIP!!

FEIGN

SIGH...22 YEARS IN HONG KONG AND IT'S FINALLY BACK HOME TO THE U.K. FOR ME.

DO YOU REALISE, MISTER SNEEDSLEY, THAT YOU'LL HAVE MISSED THE ENTIRE ERA OF THATCHER-MAJOR TORY RULE?

GOD BLESSES US IN MYSTERIOUS WAYS, MISS WONG.

YOU DESERVE IT, SIR.

AS YOUR INCOMING DEPARTMENT HEAD, I SAY WE SHOULDN'T LET MR SNEEDSLEY DEPART WITHOUT A CEREMONY.

Hong K...
Governm...
Dept. of
Prevarica...

SO LET'S GIVE HIM A SENDOFF IN THE TRUE SPIRIT OF THE HANDOVER!

FEIGN

HONG KONG'S NEW EXHIBITION CENTRE, SITE OF THE HANDOVER BANQUET.

WHERE THOUSANDS OF THE WORLD'S MOST IMPORTANT DIGNITARIES WILL GATHER FOR THIS HISTORIC FEAST.

WHERE RIGHT NOW, AS AN ARMY OF CHEFS, WAITERS AND TABLE STAFF BUSILY APPLY THE FINISHING TOUCHES, JUST ONE THOUGHT IS ON EVERYONE'S MIND...

THE BASTARDS BETTER TIP!!

PREPARING FOR THE HANDOVER BANQUET...

AND THE CHINESE LEADERS WILL BE SEATED AT THE END TABLE OVER THERE.

WHY SO FAR AWAY?

SECURITY. IF ANY PROTESTORS BARGE IN, THEY WON'T GET NEAR.

AND BESIDES...

THE SOUP WILL BE COLD BY THE TIME IT REACHES THE SONS OF BITCHES!

YOU'RE A DARING MAN, MAITRE D'!

FEIGN

HEY, COMRADE PRESIDENT JIANG. HAVING A GOOD TIME?

SPLENDID.

LISTEN — JUST SO'S WE DON'T HAVE TO BOTHER YOU LATER — WOULD YOU MIND SIGNING THIS VOUCHER FOR YOUR MEAL?

HAH? OH. SURE, SURE.

JUST GOT INDEPENDENCE FOR HONG KONG, TIBET AND TAIWAN!

DECREE

FEIGN

BALLAD OF THE HANDOVER (Karaoke version)

THE FIRST OF JULY, AN ERA BEGINS
WE RISE TO GREET THE NEW DAWN
THE SHAME OF HISTORY IS NOW AVENGED,
FINALLY THE BRITISH ARE GONE!

TRUE, HONG KONG WOULD STILL
    BE A BARREN ROCK
IF IT HADN'T BEEN OWNED BY THE BRITS,

NO ONE WOULD BE HERE,
WE'D BE BACK IN CHINA
KNEE-DEEP IN BUFFALO SHIT.

BUT NOW WE STAND PROUD:
    ONE COUNTRY UNITED!
WE RAISE OUR VOICES IN THANKS.
WELL, ANYWAY, IF WE DIDN'T
WE'D ALL BE RUN OVER BY TANKS.

FORGET ABOUT FREEDOM OF SPEECH
    AND ELECTIONS,
THEY'RE FOREIGN AS THE EASTER BUNNY.
THE FUTURE IS BRIGHT
    IF WE DO AS WE'RE TOLD:
"LET'S SHUT UP AND ALL MAKE MONEY!"

FEIGN

The Kowloon Kats

in

"The POST-1997 WEATHER REPORT"

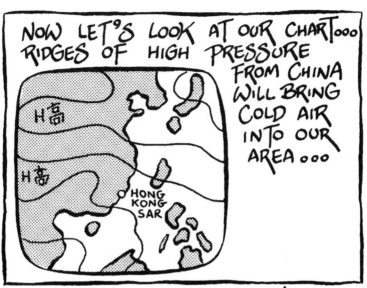

Glossary

Basic Law	mini-Constitution for Hong Kong S.A.R.
Bath	Patten's former British constituency
Canton	foreign name for Guangdung and Guangzhou
Cantonese	Chinese dialect spoken in Hong Kong
Democratic Party	pro-democracy party; HK's largest party
Deng Xiaoping	late Chinese dictator
Guangdung	province neighbouring Hong Kong
Guangzhou	major Chinese city near Hong Kong
Jiang Zemin	current Chinese dictator
Joint Declaration	1984 agreement to hand over Hong Kong
Joint Liaison Group	official Sino-British group to discuss HK issues
karaoke	Japan's revenge on the world for losing WWII
Kowloon	peninsula ceded to Britain in 1860
Major, John	former British Prime Minister
New China News Agency	*de facto* Chinese embassy in pre-1997 HK
New Territories	area leased to Britain in 1898 for 99 years
O.B.E.	Order of the British Empire; imperial honour
Opium Wars	there were two: from 1840-42 and 1856-58
Patten, Chris	last British governor of HK; loathed by China
PLA	People's Liberation Army
Provisional Legislature	body which replaced HK's elected legislature
S.A.R.	Special Administrative Region
Shenzhen	industrial zone adjacent to Hong Kong
taipan	head of major British trading firms in HK
Thatcher, Margaret	former British Prime Minister, now a Baroness
Tiananmen Square	site of massacre on 4 June 1989
Tories	Conservative Party of Great Britain
triads	Chinese criminal gangs
Wong Chuk Hang	manufacturing district in Hong Kong

By the same author

AIEEYAAA!
AIEEYAAA, Not Again!
The World of Lily Wong
Quotations From Lily Wong
The Adventures of Superlily
Postcards From Lily Wong
How The Animals Do It
Execute Yourself Tonite! (with Nury Vittachi)
Hong Kong Fairy Tales
Banned In Hong Kong
AIEEYAAA! I'm Pregnant!

---

see Lily Wong on the World Wide Web:

http://www.asiaonline.net.hk/lilywong

About Larry Feign

Born in New York, raised in California, lived in Ohio, Vermont, Massachusetts, Hawaii, Georgia, Germany and Hong Kong. Began cartooning in earnest in 1963, started getting paid for it in 1980. One wife, two children, currently no pets. Enjoys in-line skating, Thai and Italian food, Celtic traditional music and Korean ginseng wine.